A Mother So Dear

Alda Ellis

Harvest House Publishers
Eugene, Oregon 97402

A Mother So Dear
Copyright ©1998
by Harvest House Publishers
Eugene, Oregon 97402

Library of Congress Cataloging-in-Publication Data
Ellis, Alda,1952-
A mother so dear / Alda Ellis.
p. cm.
ISBN 1-56507-820-9
Mothers. 2. Mother and child. 3. Gift books.
I. Title
HQ759.E44 1998   97-40135
306.874'3—dc21   CIP

Design and production by
Left Coast Design, Portland, Oregon

Artwork which appears in this book is from
the personal collection of Alda Ellis.

Scripture quotations are from the Holy Bible, New
International Version®, Copyright © 1973, 1978, 1984 by
the International Bible Society. Used by permission of
Zondervan Publishing House.

Printed in Hong Kong
00 01 02 03 04 05 06 /NG / 10 9 8 7 6 5 4 3

*D*edicated to my sweet Daddy,
who loved my mother dearly
for all her years here on earth.

Contents

My mother was the making of me.
She was so true and so sure of me,
I felt that I had someone to live for—
someone I must not disappoint. The
memory of my mother will
always be a blessing to me.

THOMAS EDISON

*I*t seems that God has greater plans for us than we could ever dream up on our own. For it was almost a year ago, when my heart was feeling moved to share a tribute to motherhood, that I was asked to write a book about my own mother. I knew I was truly blessed with her and that God had given me one of the best mothers He ever created. Little did I know that shortly after agreeing to write a book about mothers, I would lose mine.

My mother died on the evening of her fifty-ninth wedding anniversary. My father was by her side holding her hand as he had always been. Earlier that evening, Mother had allowed all of us to say our tender good-byes

and feel complete. As I
placed my head softly on her chest
as she lay in her hospital bed, I
hugged her one last time for
this world and she hugged me back.

　　　And so it is with a saddened but
joyful heart that I now truly understand a
mother's love. For a mother's love is not something that
lasts just for a lifetime; it is something that lasts even
longer. A mother's love is truly always and forever.

A mother's love! What can compare with it!
Of all things on earth, it comes nearest to divine love in heaven.
A mother's love means a life's devotion—
And sometimes a life's sacrifice…

AUTHOR UNKNOWN

My Mother's Hands

From tiny babe
With skin so fair,
A family made
With love to share.
A treasure for all the world to see,
My mother's hands
They cradled me.

Youth passed me by,
A prom dress was bought.
Only at times it was
Her advice I sought.
Mending a heart or mending a seam,
My mother's hands
They mended me.

One boy did steal my heart away,
Mother's eyes saw what she felt in her heart
For she wished us love and never to part.
We said our vows for the world to see,
My mother's hands
They married me.

Away, apart, an empty nest,
Our fortune to make and the world to see,
A love so true, a life so blessed.
Missed and lonesome,
A phone call told whatever be,
My mother's hands
They yearned for me.

I was so busy
And had not much time
For a sweet little mother
Who was doing just fine.
Patiently she waited for a visit to be,
My mother's hands
They prayed for me.

My mother's hands
Are now laid to rest
From doing the things
That she loved best.
Gnarled and wrinkled by time I see
My mother's hands
had always loved me.

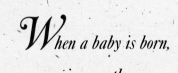

*When a baby is born,
so is a mother.*

True
happiness
be
thine

My Mother's Hands, They Cradled Me

*T*he little white frame house on Harrison Street will always be forever blessed, for that is where my mother lived. Even though Mother is gone now, that house will always be filled with cherished memories, for I can still picture her there sweeping the walk every morning, planting pansies in the springtime, and enjoying peanut-butter-and-jelly sandwich picnics with me on the back doorstep. In every room of that dear house I feel her presence. The kitchen still glistens with the floors she always waxed so shiny. The hall bespeaks of her love for family with the gallery of photographs she artistically arranged. And the bedroom, accented with her favorite shade of green, simply says "mama."

Sometimes I miss her until I ache. I wish I could again feel her kiss on my cheek. And I imagine back to one brisk, golden autumn morning some forty years ago when my daddy drove down an avenue lined with oak trees, proudly carrying his beloved wife and brand-new baby daughter home from the hospital.

It was upon looking through my mother's cedar chest that I discovered just how ready my parents were to welcome their new baby home. The wicker bassinet trimmed with yards of lace had stood ready for weeks,

fresh diapers had been neatly folded and stacked, and the baby announcement cards sat in a pile to be mailed out to family and friends. Mother and Daddy had been married ten years, and the nursery was filled with well-loved furniture that had long been in the family. They were so excited for their baby girl to be born.

> *A mother's love grows by giving.*
>
> **CHARLES LAMB**

Some forty years later, Mother and I carefully removed from the cedar chest the baby clothes she couldn't bear to part with—an elfin pair of handmade booties, a delicately cross-stitched bib, a rattle shaped like a bow, and a tiny patchwork quilt that had belonged to Mother when she was little. To my mother all of these things brought back her own memories, but to me they spoke of security, for they were precious reminders of all the love that went into each handmade stitch. The quilt, now a bit tattered and threadbare, was created not only to warm my body but also to warm my heart. Mother's lullabies were

sung to me as a melody of hope and love.

Just to touch the soft baby quilt after all these years reminds me of the blessing of a mother's touch. How miraculous a mother's touch that warms us when we are cold, feeds us when we are hungry, comforts us when we are sick, and plays games with us to put joy in our souls. Wrapping me in a warm quilt of love and devotion, my mother's hands, they cradled me.

In the sheltered simplicity of the first days after a baby is born, one sees the magical closed circle, the miraculous sense of two people existing only for each other.

ANNE MORROW LINDBERGH

15

A mother is someone
who dreams great dreams
for you, but then she lets you
chase the dreams you have for
yourself and loves you
just the same.

AUTHOR UNKNOWN

Learning How to Fly

September has always been one of my favorite months of the year. Days turned crisp, and we knew that sweater weather would soon set in. Autumn was approaching and we let summer slip from our hands. But I never minded because, to me, it is always autumn that is too precious to forget. I've heard it said that as we age we become more like our parents, and I am blessed with the comforting thought that, as the seasons turn, I shall become my mother.

September signaled a return to school, but the lessons I learned from my mother were far greater than anything school could ever teach me. Mother didn't drive a car, so she walked with me to school every day. Taller than the previous year, I held fast to my mother's hand as we sauntered along a tree-lined path until we came to a bridge over a rocky creek. From there the school ground was in sight, and Mother let go of my hand. Waving good-bye, I scurried on my way toward the schoolhouse.

After school was out for the day and I had started the walk home, I would see my mother beckoning to me in the distance. As I skipped along swinging my plaid bookbag, she stood waiting patiently for our afternoon jaunt home to begin. Preserved fondly in my personal memory book are our

conversations of those carefree school days, when I chattered on about skinned knees, games of "Red Rover" on the playground, and the day's homework assignments.

Only at times did I bring my chattering to a standstill and seek Mother's advice, but it was during those radiant passages of time that my mother and I bonded as kindred spirits. Once we both noticed some dainty pink wildflowers that were especially pretty growing beside the road. Kneeling beside them, mother's hands gently tugged the flowers from the rocky soil, and we carried them home and planted them by our gate. Today those wildflowers still bloom by the gate even though my mother doesn't live there anymore. They are a quiet reminder of the times we spent together on those crisp September afternoons. The gifts my mother gave me I did not understand as a young schoolgirl, but I now realize they were of her most valuable asset—her time.

Mother was always a source of inspiration to me. She spent many summer hours sewing new dresses for me to wear to school the coming fall. And even though they were all homemade dresses, Mother's hands adorned them with special touches of lace and a dressmaker's skilled

workmanship. Buttons from a dress outgrown made their way onto a new dress, small but cogent memories of the past. The year I turned ten, Mother kept one of the dresses back so I wouldn't see it until my early fall birthday. I was thrilled to have something new to wear to school the day I turned ten. It was just a simple dress with a gathered skirt, but to me it was much more—it was my birthday dress. To this day I cannot remember what other gifts I received on my tenth birthday, but I clearly remember the beautiful new dress—complete with a pocket on the skirt—that Mother sewed for me.

> *Whatever you do,*
> *do it with all your heart...*
>
> **THE BOOK**
> **OF COLOSSIANS**

Today sewing is a luxury for me. With my busy schedule with never enough hours in each day, I find it simply too easy to head to the mall for my children's clothing where I can pick up what they need in a matter of minutes. Besides, I could never match Mother's wonderful ability! Only now do I fully appreciate all of my mother's loving stitches that fashioned my wardrobe and mended the seams.

September's days faded to amber and signaled that

another season's bounty was ready for the harvest. In our yard stood magnificent, aged pecan trees with arms that reached for the sky. Pecans—the ones the squirrels didn't get—began to fall, and after school Mother and I picked them up off the ground and put them into our buckets. Picking up pecans meant time spent alone with Mother, when Daddy wasn't yet home from work, with just the two of us talking and laughing. As we enjoyed the crisp autumn air, Mother answered my endless stream of questions and taught me important lessons I shall never forget. One question in particular I delighted in asking her was, "What do you think I will be when I grow up?" Time after time, she gave me the same answer with a confident smile: "You can be anything you set your mind to be."

Several years later one of my junior high teachers, who was also the school football coach, assigned us to write a paper about what we might like to have as our future career. At that time airplanes fascinated me, so I

wrote my paper about becoming
a commercial airline pilot someday. I received my graded paper
back marked with an "A" and the
red-penned comment, "It is not
appropriate for a girl to seek this
career." Clearly, my mother and
my teacher had different opin-
ions on this matter.

My flying dreams were
not mentioned again until one
summer during my college years.
Mother was standing over the
stove frying okra when I announced that I wanted to take
flying lessons. Without looking up, she said, "You'll have
to use your own money." As I had not mentioned the
idea of flying in years, my revelation surprised Mother,
who perhaps had thought my airline pilot career a pass-
ing fancy. Mother had no idea what made me want to fly
now, but if I wanted to fulfill my childhood dreams, she
certainly would not stop me.

I worked long hours to pay for the flying lessons.
And it was alone on my solo flight—just God and me up

high in the clouds—that I realized I could be nearly any-thing I wanted to be. Mother's lessons were remembered well, for not even a teacher could give better advice. Although perhaps I no longer wished to be the commercial airline pilot of my junior high dreams, here I was "soloing" in the clouds. I *could* fly if I wanted to. Thank you, Mother, for all the years of encouraging me and teaching me how to "fly."

> *It seems to me that my mother was*
> *the most splendid woman I ever knew....*
> *If I have amounted to anything, it will be due to her.*
>
> CHARLIE CHAPLIN

My mother, moreover, succeeded in making me understand a good deal…. Indeed, I owe to her loving wisdom all that was bright and good in my long night.

HELEN KELLER

Messages
of Love

Although my parents never had very much
money, they blessed me with priceless trea-
sures and gifts. Two of the greatest gifts my mother passed
on to me were a love of books and a heart for music. How
well I recall her hands turning the pages of a book or play-
ing a chord on the piano.

For as long as I can remember, Mother read to me.
Accompanied by the rhythmic "click, click" of the old-fash-
ioned rocking chair we sat in together, I read with her, safe

and secure in her arms. Mother's days were always filled with tasks, but somehow she always found time to rock me and read me a story before I fell asleep each night. *Old Mother Goose, Peter Rabbit,* and *Down on the Farm* she read to me completely from memory. As I turned the pages—sometimes too early, sometimes too late—Mother never missed a word. Often I would fall asleep in her arms, her affectionate hugs giving me a stronghold for life.

In a prominent corner of our cozy, middle-class living room, next to the "new" but used piano, sat a large cardboard box that Mother had covered with pretty shelf paper. Perfectly placed in my own personal corner of the room, the box was filled with books that opened the door to faraway places I could only hope to one day visit. To this very day, my

two sons know that my favorite kind of days are rainy days, for they give me a good excuse to curl up with the warm companionship of a favorite book while leaving the world behind.

Going to the library with Mother inspired those journeys of the spirit. On library days Mother and I walked the two blocks from our home to the bus stop, then rode the bus to the town library. Walking the two blocks home from the bus stop presented me with a real challenge, for I had my arms filled with all the books they could carry. To nourish and inspire my imagination, Mother helped me choose just the right kind to read—*The Five Little Peppers, Rebecca of Sunnybrook Farm,* and my favorite, *Little Women*. But I insisted on carrying the books all by myself.

More than a patron of literature though, Mother was a Christian who lived her life by the one true Book and shared her faith daily. On those long bus rides to and from the library, we discussed lessons of faith. Perhaps Mother shared a lesson on honesty, or a bit about courage, or

perhaps her favorite lesson—never to repeat anything you might later be sorry you said. "You can never be sorry for something you did not say," she would remind me time and again. And she modeled a shining example of her words, closing her ears to the neighbors' idle gossip.

Another lesson I learned from Mother was that of courage, for after having read one too many mystery novels I was tormented by scary dreams. Sitting on the edge of my bed at night, Mother calmed my fears and reminded me that I was never alone—Jesus was always right there beside me. To this day, those reassuring words of hers still comfort me.

Then came the day when I needed more than just Mother's words—I needed her actions to save me. Our fluffy yellow Easter chick had grown into a full-fledged, regal red-and-green rooster that struck fear even in the hearts of the biggest neighborhood dogs. That rooster intimidated anyone and anything that came into our fenced-in yard, for that was *his* territory.

I can remember standing at the screen door, waiting for the precise moment to make a run for the swingset when the rooster wasn't looking. Running as if my life depended on it (and I really thought it did!), I would sprint across the lawn, then hop into the swingset and swing so high that the rooster couldn't get me. But it was a battle of the wills as he stood at attention, eyes fixed on me in my swingset, for what seemed like hours. Tired of swinging by now, I wanted my mother! She couldn't hear me calling her, and I just knew I couldn't make it to the house faster than the rooster. With my heart pounding, I jumped off the swing and hit the ground running, rooster trailing close behind. I can still remember his outstretched wings and his sharp beak. Then I saw Mother, broom in hand, preparing to sweep our walk. The rooster met his match with my mother and her broom. Feathers were flying and I was screaming, but I was safe with my head buried in Mother's skirt. Just touching her skirt, I knew everything was okay.

That was the last time I saw our territorial rooster, for Mother had Daddy take him to a friend who lived in the country. Under the oak-tree bough, my beloved swingset hideaway was safe again. I could once again sit placidly in my swing and read my book for as long as I liked because, with

Mother's help and quick hands, I had won the battle.

Besides accompanying me to the library and heading off roosters with brooms, my mother blessed me with another priceless gift—a heart for music. It is only now that I realize that this gift, too, was a sacrifice. Piano lessons taught by the town piano teacher, Mrs. Wilson, filled my after-school hours. The money for the piano lessons was very hard for my parents to come by, but somehow Mother always was able to juggle the family budget enough to keep the lessons coming.

Guarding my infancy,
Guiding my youth,
Leading me, teaching me
Lessons of truth.
Gifts were of music,
Good books, and dear friends—
All from my mother,
whose love I now send.

Because Mother never learned to drive a car, a tall glass of iced tea and a piece of fresh apple cake sitting temptingly on our dining room table persuaded Mrs. Wilson to give my piano lessons at our home. A recent widow, Mrs. Wilson played the organ at the baseball field and the organ at our church. Not surprisingly, she ended each of my piano lessons with a "hymn of the week" for me to learn. Those hymns are forever etched in my heart,

for although I may not remember all the words to them, I caught myself humming their melodies time and again in my front porch swing while I soothed my baby boys to sleep.

It's been years since I have played the piano, but my lessons of music were given selflessly, and they enriched my entire being. Now my two sons are taking violin lessons of their own. I don't necessarily expect to produce a concert violinist, but I do want to plant seeds of joy in their spirit and touch their souls with music as my dear mother and faithful Mrs. Wilson touched mine.

Mrs. Wilson is still our church organist, and last Sunday my oldest son played "Amazing Grace" on his violin as she accompanied him. Even though my mother was not sitting in the pews, I'm sure she and the angels were watching from above and smiling at the joyful sound.

When you looked into my mother's eyes,
you knew as if He told you why God sent her
into the world. It was to open the minds
of all who looked to beautiful thoughts.

J.M. BARRIE

"I favour the smell
of sweet grass," he said.
"It always makes me
think of my mother."

L. M. MONTGOMERY

Along the Shore

Pickles in the Pantry

For as long as I can remember, my mother canned pickles. Sweet pickles, bread-and-butter pickles, dill pickles—rarely was a meal ever served at our house that didn't include Mother's homemade pickles.

Not even the smallest step was forgotten when my mother made pickles. Each jar was properly scalded and readied. The cucumbers were grown from Mother's beloved kitchen garden, and after they had soaked adequately in the brine that filled an army of crocks and dishpans, they could be packed in jars one by one with Mother's careful hands and tightly sealed. Each jar truly represented a labor of love.

With pride Mother took the pickles to my father's family reunion. Potluck suppers at church were always blessed with one of her pickle jars. And years and years of summer picnics were all made even sunnier by Mother's special pickles.

One particular summer evening Mother and I were together in the kitchen, having just finished washing and drying the dinner dishes. She was lifting the corner of a neatly placed dishtowel to take another peek at the dozen or so pickle jars cooling on the stove. Her labor evidenced by a Band-Aid wrapped around a burned finger and an aggravating splinter stubbornly stuck in her hand, she awkwardly carried on her tasks. At the same moment Mother was raising the dishtowel, the young man who had stolen my heart was sitting nervously in our living room, asking my daddy if he could marry me.

With Daddy's "yes" secured, a fall wedding was planned and the preparation began. Mother spent endless

hours sewing. Bridal showers were given and thank-you notes written.

My future in-laws invited us over for a celebration dinner where, of course, Mother brought a prize jar of her pickles for the grand occasion.

Over the years my husband taught me to appreciate Mother's treat that I had so long taken for granted. The homemade pickles were of a bygone era, and I never seemed to find the time or desire to make them myself. But tuna fish sandwiches tasted better with Mama's pickles, my husband's grilled hamburgers weren't complete without them, and a proper Christmas dinner always included a dish of the homemade pickles.

Right now I have a jar of Mother's pickles displayed in my pantry. I don't know when—or if—I will ever open them. For every time I look at them, my saddened heart aches for my mother's company. I think of the wonderful influence she had on my two small sons, and how she wholeheartedly shared my joys and my sorrows. I'd always felt comfort in knowing that I could pick up the telephone any time to ask her opinion on any subject, and she often kindly just listened to me as I rambled on. She was my dear friend, and I miss the gifts of time and energy she so generously gave.

My childhood gifts to her—a lopsided plaster handprint plate, a dimestore-bought bird figurine, a red rose vase—unfailingly assumed a place of honor in Mother's living room. She owned much nicer keepsakes to display, and I never could quite understand why she insisted on displaying my clumsy gifts instead. But I have a feeling that, years from now, Mother will understand why a jar of her homemade pickles still sits proudly in my pantry.

Mother,
As long ago we carried to your knees
The tales and treasures of eventful days,
Knowing no deed too humble for your praise,
Nor any gift too trivial to please,
So still we bring with older smiles and tears,
What gifts we may to claim the old, dear right;
Your faith beyond the silence and the night;
Your love still close and watching through the years.

AUTHOR UNKNOWN

$\mathcal{M}$y mother

was the source from which

I derived the guiding

principles of my life.

JOHN WESLEY

My Mother's Hands, They Prayed for Me

The first step to wisdom is silence, the second is listening. Although my mother never spoke those words, she didn't have to; she practiced them daily. And at times it had to be difficult for her, especially as I think of how she kept my father calm in the midst of his teenage daughters' hectic social lives. And then I think of when my Mother sprung a surprise of her own on Daddy.

Mother and Daddy were simple people—one car, one telephone, one television set. Yet through the years my

39

mother never ceased to amaze me. Despite her outward simplicity, she was anything but predictable.

Mother ran an organized, thrifty, and tidy household, but she was forever surprising us with an unexpected new interest of hers. Her faith and family always came first, but she always had something "cookin" on the back burner. I remember the time she persuaded my

> *In all my efforts to learn to read, my mother shared fully my ambition and sympathized with me and aided me in every way she could. If I have done anything in life worth attention, I feel sure that I inherited the disposition from my mother.*
>
> **BOOKER T. WASHINGTON**

father that she could teach kindergarten while my sister and I were in school. She taught for three years until the little neighborhood kindergarten moved to another location. One summer she decided she could paint the inside of our house all by herself. So she did, complete with a pink-hued kitchen. Some thirty years ago she signed up for a beginning computer class. After graduating from the course, she told me it was something she could fall back on "just in case of hard times." The machine she learned on

was a dinosaur of a computer, and she would bring its punched manila cards home from class for us to see. My daddy just shook his head and smiled. Daddy was very patient with Mother, up until the day she announced she was going to learn to drive.

I was in college at the time, and my classes were almost within walking distance of our house so I lived at home. I remember coming home from school one evening and sitting down to a silent dinner table where the usually flowing conversation was almost nonexistent. I couldn't imagine the reason for the tension in the air, for Mother and Daddy rarely disagreed. (Or, now that I look back, I realize that perhaps they did disagree, but one would always bite their tongue!) Hurriedly I ate my meal,

then excused myself to my part-time job at a local department store. How I loved that job! It was great fun to be surrounded by so many beautiful clothes and to be able to visit with the pleasant customers. And I was especially eager to get there on this particular night.

When I returned home from work I learned what Mother and Daddy's argument had been about. My boyfriend, who is now my husband, had decided to teach Mother to drive. Like Daddy, I couldn't believe my ears. Why learn to drive now, after all these years? But my Mother had fed this polite young man her scrumptious dinners night after night, so I am sure he was an obliging participant in the scheme.

True to her nature, Mother read her Bible and pored over the scriptures in search of guidance about learning to drive. I'm sure she believed she was doing God's will no matter what obstacles she encountered, my father included. Yet, to my Mother, being a faithful and loving spouse meant not only having courage and faith, but also patience and a desire to keep learning and growing.

A short time later, during another "light conversation" dinner, Mother announced that she had passed her

driver's test. "Well, just what do you plan to do with it?" Daddy asked. "You know we only have one car." Mother quietly replied, "Well, you just might need me to take you somewhere someday."

As the years passed by, Mother drove to the beauty shop once a week. That was the only time she needed the car—until the day that Daddy had heart problems and Mother rushed him to the hospital. He needed to have surgery, and every day of his two-week stay Mother drove the car to visit him in the hospital.

One of my favorite pictures in my

> *I remember my mother's prayers, and they have always followed me. They have clung to me all of my life.*
>
> **ABRAHAM LINCOLN**

wedding album is a photo of Mother waving good-bye to my new husband and me as we leave the church, bound for our honeymoon. Daddy is standing next to Mother with his arm around her. It must have been a difficult moment for her as she cut the threads she had so gently woven. Someday I too will find out just how she felt. And, following my mother's shining example of faithfully seeking the will of God, I pray already for dear, sweet daughters-in-

law who will one day marry my sons. Looking back, I reflect upon how my Mother touched the heart of God with her tender Mother's prayer.

The prayers of my Mother guided my way throughout my life. How thankful I am she loved me enough to place me in God's great care.

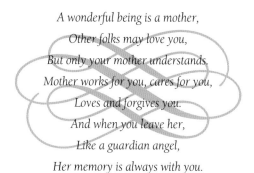

A wonderful being is a mother,
Other folks may love you,
But only your mother understands.
Mother works for you, cares for you,
Loves and forgives you.
And when you leave her,
Like a guardian angel,
Her memory is always with you.

AUTHOR UNKNOWN

44

Epilogue

Mother was well known for her made-from-scratch, homemade-crust pecan pies. She knew that the true secret for happiness was in doing something for others—whether it was baking pies or giving hugs—and the way she lived her life illustrated this.

When Mother Teresa was awarded the Nobel Peace Prize, the selfless nun was asked, "What can we do to promote world peace?" Mother Teresa replied, "Go home and love your family." And that is the advice my mother took to heart, living and loving it each day.

From the moment she took me home from the hospital as a tiny baby to the day when her familiar hands bade me farewell after my wedding, Mother loved me. I learned from her that I don't have to build grand cathedrals to become great. Instead, I can achieve my own greatness by lovingly building Christian character in my two sons.

In my mother's rocking chair I have rocked my two

sons to sleep. My heartfelt prayers are that I will teach them to "fly," keep them from the "roosters," and plant the seeds of joy—nurtured by good books and beautiful music—in their souls.

Mother used to sit at the foot of my bed at night, telling me that I could ask her anything. When I was a small child, I was certain she could answer any of my questions. But as I grew older and my questions became more difficult, that certainty disappeared and Mother directed me toward God, who *did* have all the answers.

Oh, I have been most fortunate to have been blessed with such a mother, for not everyone has been so blessed. It makes me feel very humble to imagine that God thought I was so deserving to have been blessed with a mother so dear.

Thank you, Mother, for my yesterdays as you held me tight in the palm of your hand, and may my tomorrows be spent with God safe in the palm of His hand.

The memory of the righteous will be a blessing...

THE BOOK OF PSALMS

47

*You know that nothing can
ever change what we have always been
and always will be to each other.*

FRANKLIN ROOSEVELT
To his mother, 1911

*A mother's love for the child of her body differs
essentially from all other affections, and burns with so
steady and clear a flame that it appears like the one
unchangeable thing in this earthly mutable life, so
that when she is no longer present it is still a
light to our steps and a consolation.*

W.H. HUDSON